"The Master Builder: Renty Tucker
learned his craft as a slave,
but made his mark as a free man"

~Charles Swenson,
Coastal Observer, 02/19/15

April 21, 2018
To Jessilen & John Clark
who will make this world
a better place,
Love,
[Re & S- Dad]

Renty's Bell

The Story of Renty Tucker (1831-1913),
A Remarkable All-but-Forgotten South Carolinian

Robert D. Insley

COVER: Prince George Winyah Episcopal Church,
Georgetown, SC

ISBN: 978-1-941069-57-8

Published by Prose Press
Pawleys Island, South Carolina
prosencons@live.com

ACKNOWLEDGMENTS

With love and respect, I would like to thank my wife Claudia, for her encouragement, patience, and assistance during this undertaking.

I am grateful for so many others that I approached who were enthusiastic and willing to share their knowledge, skills, and encouragement:

Patti Burns of the Georgetown County Library System took this novice by the hand and patiently taught me the basics of genealogical research and digital research of periodicals.

Dr. Hal and Mrs. Margaret Holmes for sharing their beautiful collection of Emily Weston's art work and collaborating as new information surfaced.

Mrs. Corinne Taylor, current owner and steward of the Pelican Inn for allowing me to explore the structural and architectural details of this historic treasure.

David Evans former owner and steward of the Pelican for sharing artifacts and details that he and his family discovered during their long ownership.

Steve Banta of PI Woodworks for sharing his knowledge of historic restoration.

Historians Charles Joyner as well as Anthony Devereux who gave me early encouragement to pursue this story.

Mrs. Joyce Tucker McIntosh, Renty's great granddaughter, who shared with me her knowledge of recent family history.

William Stevens , forensic anthropologist, for sharing his data and knowledge of the remains unearthed at the St. Mary's Hagley cemetery site.

Angela Lawrimore for her extensive pro bono title searching services.

Charles Swenson of the *Coastal Observer* for featuring my summary article.

Mary Boyd of the Georgetown County Museum and archivist for Prince George Church.

Annie Pott , professional proofreader.

Probate Judge Waldo Maring.

Pat Wylie, Verger of Grace Episcopal Church.

Tom Stickler, Pres. Hagley Estates POA

My Publisher, Bob O'Brien of Prose Press for walking me through this new world of getting a book published.

And to all the others who took the time to speak with me regarding this topic which almost always gave me new insight.

I. Introduction

I first read the name Renty Tucker in Charles Joyner's *Down by the Riverside* (1984). Professor Joyner's work is considered the most comprehensive research ever published on the slave community of the Waccamaw Neck rice culture that flourished during the nineteenth century in Georgetown County, South Carolina. Renty Tucker was a highly skilled carpenter enslaved at Hagley Plantation.

Plowden C.J. Weston, the owner of Hagley and Weehawka, an adjacent plantation, was married to Emily Frances Esdaile, originally from England. Tucker had built the Westons' palatial summer home on Pawleys Island, now known as "The Pelican Inn." He also built a slave chapel that served the enslaved African American Hagley people as well as those from Weehawka. This chapel, named St. Mary's, could seat around 300 worshipers and was quite possibly the most elaborate and elegant slave chapel ever constructed anywhere in the South.

As I began researching Renty Tucker's story, both during slavery and especially after emancipation, I discovered what a long and notable life he had lived. During his entire adult life, he provided for his spouses as well as numerous children and grandchildren. He became a respected and beloved civic leader in Georgetown County, serving as county coroner and as a member of the

Georgetown City Board of Health. He was an active member and sexton of Prince George Winyah Episcopal Church. He was the founder and builder of a humble but beautiful church in Georgetown, created so that emancipated African Americans who wished to do so, could continue worshiping as Episcopalians, the primary denomination during the time of slavery in the Waccamaw region of the county.

Renty's remains were interred with honors at Prince George Winyah, a church known to also have served a significant number of affluent white parishioners. In addition, he accrued a modest amount of wealth, leaving a valuable estate to his heirs. In some ways he achieved what some may call "The American Dream," in spite of the seemingly insurmountable challenges of living as a former slave during reconstruction and into the Jim Crow Era.

Renty Tucker; a most remarkable man, has almost been forgotten by all but a few Georgetonians.

II. Renty Tucker's Origins

The first U.S. Census that included formerly enslaved African Americans, was taken in 1870. It was the first decennial census after emancipation. Prior to emancipation, slaveholders provided the U.S. Census Bureau with a slave "inventory." Names were not provided; just age and gender. The U.S. Constitution allowed slaves to be counted as 3/5 of a person towards the general population for the purpose of reapportionment of U.S. Representatives. This is one of the reasons that African Americans who wish to trace their lineage and learn more of their genealogies encounter many "walls."

On his first U.S. Census, Renty Tucker's birth year was recorded as 1842. This was a mistake on someone's part. On each successive census, as well as in other documents until his death, his birth date was recorded as July, 1831, with his birthplace listed as South Carolina.

In the summer of 1862, it was almost impossible to send mail from overseas into the South during the Civil War. Reverend William W. Malet, Emily Weston's brother-in-law, traveled from England and visited Hagley with news of the death of Emily's mother. Rev. Malet later published the diary of his trip as *An Errand to the South in the Summer of 1862* (London, 1863). In his notes, he stated that "all of the 350 negroes except Pembra (about 70 yrs who was brought over from Africa as a child) were born on the estate" [*sic*].

The subject of family, or last names of slaves is an interesting one. It is a common myth that enslaved African Americans usually took the surname of their owner. In February of 1871, Renty Tucker opened a savings account with the Freedman's Bank. On the application he stated that his parents' names were Ben and Delia (Tucker), both deceased. His signature on this application appears in perfect cursive script with a beautiful fluid stroke. On the 1900 census, it was recorded that both of Renty's parents had been born in South Carolina. An *ancestry.com* search shows that his mother, Delia, was born about 1795 and, in 1855 at the age of 60, was an infirmary nurse on Laurel Hill (another Weston family plantation located on present day Brookgreen Gardens property). Transcripts from *ancestry.com* also show that Tucker had one brother named Summer (or possibly Samuel?), who died in 1864. He had four sisters: Nancy, Harriet, Mary Ann, and Salena. Not much has been found concerning Renty's father, Ben.

During his visit, Malet baptized Renty's infant daughter, "Dido" (Adeline). He stated in his diary that Renty and Josephine, Renty's wife, used the "title" of Tucker, and that the slaves had family names but seldom used them except among themselves. Elizabeth Collins, an English housekeeper hired by the Westons, in referring to slave "titles," wrote that: "I have often noticed they use them among themselves" (*Memories of the Southern*

States, 1865). Malet (1863) recorded that there was a footman named Gabriel who had the family name of Knox. Mary, a housemaid, had the "title" of Green. Historian Anthony Devereux, in "*The Rice Princess-A Rice Epoch Revisited*" (1973), writes that after emancipation the more popular names assumed for Hagley were Grant and Wigfall. The names of Blake, Washington, and Green were also popular. Devereux was told that there was only one known descendent from the Hagley people who adopted the Weston name, John O. Weston. Mr. W.H. "Bill" Murray, formerly of Sandy Island, now living on the mainland with his wife Betty, both in their nineties, recalls John O. Weston well, as John O. Weston served as Mrs. Murray's godparent. (Sadly, Mr. Murray passed away in October, 2015)

Emily's appraisal of the estate in 1864 (Plowden Weston died in 1864 and Emily returned to England), as well as earlier Weston family papers, listed Renty Tucker only as "Renty- good carpenter and house servant," and his wife "Josephine- washer and seamstress." Renty used the Tucker name prior to emancipation. I have found only one reference to slave owners on the Waccamaw neck with the surname of Tucker; Dr. John Hyrne Tucker (1775-1859) and his two sons, also doctors, who inherited Willbrook and Litchfield plantations. Interestingly, Plowden's great aunt was John H. Tucker's daughter.

George C. Rogers, Jr., in "*The History of Georgetown County South Carolina*" (1970), states that the wealthy rice planter families in the Waccamaw region (Tuckers,

Alstons, Westons, Heriots, and Wards) frequently intermarried. My best guess is that Renty Tucker or his elders may have adopted the Tucker family name as a result of this connection with the John Tucker family. Mr. Murray told me that Tucker is a common last name for slave descendants still living on Sandy Island.

A question that requires further study is why did plantation owners refrain from using family names for slaves and consistently refer to them only by first names? When two slaves listed on a plantation inventory had the same first names, there were designations such as "Old Nancy" and "Tom's Nancy" to distinguish the two. I can only speculate and ask, "Could it be, that by discouraging and not recognizing family names for slaves, their owners could avoid the uncomfortable reminder that, when selling a slave, you are likely separating family members?"

During this research project, I believe that I have come to know Mr. Renty Tucker almost intimately, and I mean no disrespect when referring to him occasionally as simply "Renty." I feel that his first name has character. The origin of the first name Renty is unclear. I have occasionally found others named Renty on various slave records, so this first name was not unheard of. The only reference to the origin of the name Renty that I have found is a small 6-square mile settlement of around 525 people (2006) in the most northwest region of France, Nord-Pas-de-Calais. Tucker is a fairly common surname; fortunately, by Renty having an uncommon first name, my research has been somewhat simplified.

III. Renty Tucker's Accomplishments as a Carpenter

One of the many things I admire about this man is his mastery of the building arts. If one examines the architectural and structural details of Pawleys Island's "Pelican Inn," it becomes very evident that, at the relatively young age of 26 or 27, Renty Tucker had already achieved the status of a master craftsman.

Joyner (1984) writes that Renty Tucker was one of the most talented carpenters in All Saints Parish, and it was said that he had been trained in fine carpentry in England. In some cases, it is known that slaves were sent to Charleston or even England to be taught particular skills, such as cabinetry. Apparently, no documentation has been found to prove this trip occurred. Elizabeth Collins (1865) writes that the Westons traveled to England about every two years during their marriage. The only possible evidence substantiating that Renty trained in England, that I have been able to locate, is a newspaper announcement of passengers departing to England. The May 26, 1848 *American and Commercial Daily Advertiser* (Baltimore, MD) announced, in part, "In the steamship Cambria, sailed from New York on Wednesday for Liverpool: Mr. Plowden

C.J. Weston, lady and servant" were on board. Another research "wall," as slaves were rarely, if ever, named on passenger lists.

Commonly, senior craftspeople took on younger slaves who showed a particular interest or a talent, as apprentices. Carpenters were regularly trained on the plantation. Thomas Bonneau was a slave and master carpenter for Robert F.W. Allston (1801-1864). Bonneau reportedly stated in a prideful manner that he did not send out "jack-legs" (Joyner, 1984). It is possible that Tucker apprenticed under Bonneau. There were many other "prized" slave carpenters known on the Waccamaw Neck, and I can only speculate as to whom Tucker might have trained under. I have also not found the names of any young people that Tucker mentored, as he surely must have. Renty Tucker was commonly sent, unsupervised, with a crew of carpenters under his direction, to various locales around All Saints Parish (Joyner, 1984). Good carpenters were in demand and were able to hire out to other plantations, paying a portion of their profit to their masters and keeping the balance. There is a record of James Sparkman hiring a carpenter for a time and paying $120, which would be approximately 2 times the cost of a horse (Joyner, 1984). It was quite an accomplishment when one considers the numerous "big houses", slave quarters, chapels, summer cottages, rice mills, barns, stables, and workshops, as well as rice trunks that were built. The overwhelming evidence, from old illustrations, as well as the buildings that survived, shows a highly-developed level of skill and craftsmanship.

It is even more admirable when considering the relatively simple hand tools that were employed during that period of American rural development. Renty, and at least three of his sons, Josiah, St. Julian, and Henry, continued as carpenters. At this writing, homebuilder and carpenter Daniel Grate of Pawleys Island, talked with me about his ancestors tracing back to slavery days. All the men in his line continued in the trade; father and grandfather mentoring their children and grandchildren.

Concerning the Westons' summer residence, Elizabeth Collins stated in her diary (1865), that it was "a summer residence lately built by Renty. I can only compare this building to a castle so lofty that we could find a cool place almost in any part of the house." Plowden and Emily did not name this home "The Pelican Inn"; that name came from a more recent owner. Their name for this summer home and the original 5.5 acres that it stood on was "Weston Zoyland", named for an English village near Emily's home in Somerset, UK.

"Weston Zoyland 1860", Sketch by Emily Weston *Image from website of Bonhams Auctions, London

The property was purchased by Weston around 1844. In 1846, Governor Robert F.W. Allston's slaves constructed the South Causeway. At the time it was known as Allston's Bank, and is believed to be the oldest causeway in continuous use in South Carolina. Hagley became a busy and productive community. There were various workshops and service outbuildings where blacksmithing, carpentry, boatbuilding, and agricultural work were performed. By the mid to late 1850's, the stage was set for the construction of a magnificent summer cottage to escape from the heat and malarial mosquitoes on the mainland. The building was constructed primarily of heart pine, probably hewn in the carpentry shop at Hagley and then transported to the island. The original roofing was of shake shingles most likely cypress.

Roman numerals were commonly chiseled in cut lumber during this period. It is speculated that these numbers assisted in the proper assembly of structural elements, and is supporting evidence that Tucker prefabricated some of the structural elements in his workshop back on the mainland. Daniel Grate, who worked with his father, told me about being under the Pelican Inn and marveling at the length of the timbers, some of which "were at least 30 feet." Assembly was accomplished with wooden pegs, cut nails, and mortise and tenon joints. The elegant Gothic-style pointed arches, almost a signature of Renty Tucker's work, can be seen in the surrounding porches. A previous owner covered these arches, presumably to increase shade.

Later owners, the Evans family, restored these essential details, around 1993.

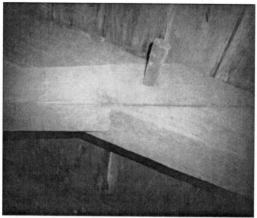

Example of original joinery in the roof framing of the
Pelican Inn (Photo by Author)

Present Day "Pelican Inn" (Photograph by the Author)

In 1858, the Westons were planning the construction of a large slave chapel. Starting in the early part of 1859, Renty Tucker must have been immersed in this project. It has been written that he first constructed a scale model (Joyner, 1984), presumably to confirm that the proportions were architecturally correct. The Westons ordered very elaborate architectural and religious elements from England, the quality of which were unavailable in America at the time. They obtained stained glass windows, carved oak stalls, and an English sandstone baptismal font quarried, then carved, near Emily's birthplace. In addition, a gold chalice for Holy Communion and a clock and bell for the tower were included in the imported shipment.

Construction commenced in early 1859. By the time the Westons returned from England at the end of November, 1859, Tucker had erected the church tower. By the spring of 1860, the stained-glass lancet windows and the clock and chimes had arrived. A formal opening occurred later that spring (Joyner, 1984). I am curious as to how he knew the exact proportions for framing these components, or did he simply leave rough openings until the shipment arrived?

In the summer of 1862, Rev. William W. Malet described St. Mary's as a pretty wooden church with lancet windows, double walls about three feet wide and in the tower a "capital" clock (An English expression meaning splendid). Malet also writes that the thick double walls were to ensure coolness inside the chapel. Reverend Henry D. Bull, All Saints pastor from 1925-1953, using parish records in his book, *All Saints Church, Waccamaw*

1739-1968-The Parish, The Place, The People (1968), writes that, "The chapel was cruciform in shape, had a high deep chancel, the transepts were deep and high." He wrote further that, "It was no mere preaching hall, but the creation of someone who had poured upon it good taste, reverence, and a love of beauty."

Copy of original sketch by Emily Weston entitled; "St Mary's Chapel, Hagley-1862" Courtesy of Dr. Hal and Mrs. Margaret Holmes

Rendering of the Interior of St. Mary's Chapel, Hagley. Source: Devereux (1973)- Courtesy Anthony Devereux

With the death of Plowden in 1864 and Emily returning to her English homeland, the chapel became neglected. Plowden's friend and cousin, William St. Julian Mazyck of Charleston, inherited the property with the stipulation of providing Emily an "...annuity of Four hundred and twenty pounds Sterling (£420)" for life. I feel that Tucker must have had a favorable relationship with William St. Julian Mazyck, as Renty and Josephine named one of their sons St. Julian. (This assumes that enslaved parents at Hagley had input in the naming of their children. Most authorities agree that the owners choose the first names for their slaves, especially if they were newly arrived and purchased for the first time. There is evidence that some enslaved parents chose their children's names but it may have involved the owner's consent. The names were most often of British or European origin but classical, biblical, literary, calendar, African, geographic, status, virtue, aspirational, and historical first names are all commonly found in the record)

Following the Civil War, with the absence of slave labor and the decline of large scale rice production, the church and surrounding grounds continued to decline. Sometime around 1866 -67, Mazyck, concerned about the fate of St. Mary's, began to have the valuable components dismantled and donated these items to other Parish churches in the region (Bull, 1968). The magnificent English stained glass windows can now be admired above the altar and over the side doors of Prince George Winyah Episcopal Church in Georgetown. They also accepted the bell and clock from the church tower, as well as the gold communion chalice. English oak stalls, locks, and other ornamental elements went to Prince Fredrick's Pee Dee in the Plantersville section of Georgetown County. The English quarried and carved baptismal font went to Grace Church, Camden. I believe that Tucker likely played a significant role in the removal and reinstallation of these church components, as no one was more qualified or more intimately familiar with the chapel. Rev. Henry D. Bull (1968) wrote that Renty Tucker moved the bell from St. Mary's to Prince

George Winyah, and later became sexton of Prince George Church where he rang the bell every Sunday. When Renty Tucker died and his body was buried at Prince George Church, Rev. Bull (1968) stated that "the bell was tolled for his funeral".

English stained glass originally from St. Mary's Hagley.
Now behind the alter at Prince George Winyah
(Photograph by Author)

21

A photograph was taken around 1915 showing the slave cemetery and the chapel. It is evident that the tower had been reclaimed and there was evidence of apparent roof damage. It is not surprising, considering the magnitude of the hurricanes that devastated the Waccamaw region in 1893, then again in 1906, as well as how quickly wood structures decay in the humid South Carolina Lowcountry if neglected. Sometime around 1930, St. Mary's burned down in a forest fire (Bull, 1968). During the early 1970's, I personally examined what was left of the old slave cemetery on the river bluff approximately 1/10 of a mile south of Hagley Landing. There were still some remaining headstones. A few conch shells had been left on the gravesites, presumably a slave custom. I could find no evidence of the chapel, which we know was located at the same site. Riverfront property, especially with the spectacular view from the bluff, is choice real estate. The site is now populated with large luxury homes. In 2006, during construction of a home on this site, skeletal remains were uncovered during excavation. The remains were removed by construction workers and the coroner was contacted a day or so later. The coroner collected the bones which were comingled. The remains had already lost all context or association of the buried individuals; another example of why the written story of slave history is so fragmented, and how historic and religious sites can be so easily lost to development. William Stevens, a doctoral student in biological anthropology at the University of South Carolina, is currently studying these remains in a dissertation project focused on reconstructing their lifestyles during enslavement. The long term goal is to respectfully inter these remains in an appropriate site that will remain as a permanent memorial.

Photograph St. Mary's Hagley ca. 1915, Courtesy of William Stevens

One occasionally hears that while trying to answer a question by conducting research, the answers are found but the study often leads to new questions. I found this to be true. My primary intent was to tell the story of Renty Tucker. History is not one isolated event or story, but are many interconnected to other related stories. It is tempting to stray from the original scope of a project when interesting and related facts are uncovered. Towards the end of my initial research, I began to pull on a different loose thread from the same piece of fabric. I began to wonder, where did the majority of the approximately 300 Hagley slaves settle after emancipation? We know that it was common for Waccamaw Neck planters to provide some land on the estate for former slaves. The original Weston estate did not stop at US 17 (Ocean Highway) as does the present Hagley Estates subdivision. Hagley Plantation originally stretched from the Waccamaw River and its marshes across the "neck" to the ocean. Today, there is a small African American community called Marysville (sometimes locally pronounced as "Maysville"), just south of the South Causeway and adjacent to and east of US 17 North. Directly across the highway from the settlement is the community church, St. Mary's AME. Both are located on the former Weston/Mazyck estate.

Both Malet (1863) and Devereux (1973), write that some of the most common family names taken by the Hagley slaves were; Knox, Green, Grant, Wigfall, Blake and Washington. Most of these are also the most common names found in today's Marysville community, along with others such as Alston and Mazyck. I talked with two senior members of the community, and both told me that they recalled their elders saying they had descended from the Hagley people.

It seems reasonable to think that when the beautiful St. Mary's Chapel was no longer available for worship, a new church would be erected at the new settlement and also named St. Mary's. Even the community name provides a tempting clue to this possible connection. The congregation recently celebrated their 50th anniversary in the present chapel, built in 1964. Several community members over 55 years old told me that they remember the former chapel just north of the present location. All said that they remember that it was very old and of wood frame construction. Mr. W.H. "Bill" Murray told me he clearly remembered visiting the building in the late 1930's and early 40's, prior to his entering the U.S. Navy, and it contained very old "hand-hewn" timbers (his words). Could former slaves have deconsecrated (not desecrated) portions of the chapel and reconsecrated a church in their new village? These were difficult economic times and new building materials were cost-prohibitive. At best, this is merely a hypothesis and something a more qualified and discerning student of history may one day wish to pursue.

Renty Tucker's amazing story is far from over. Tucker remained on the Waccamaw Neck until at least February, 1871. On his 1871 bank application, Tucker stated that he was a carpenter employed by a John Richardson. I do not know if Renty was acting as an independent builder or if he was a more traditional employee. There is a record of a John Richardson, a Reconstruction era land owner, of nearby Waterford Plantation.

The Freedman's Bureau Act of March, 1865, allowed planters to keep their plantations if they took an oath of allegiance to the United States. Land owners who took the oath were to inform their former slaves, who had remained on the plantation, that they were free. The land owner could enter into a legal contract with those who wished to remain and work. The planter was to provide essential provisions until crops or livestock were harvested, or for at least 60 days (Rogers, 1970). The freedmen were to receive one-half of the crop. A representative from the federal troops occupying the Georgetown district was to approve the contract and determine if it was equitable. The federal troops were to insure fair compliance, as well. If owners chose not to plant or cultivate, then former slaves from that plantation were permitted to establish settlements on the land. William St. Julian Mazyck, the new owner of Hagley plantation, took the oath on July 22, 1865. We know that Tucker remained on the Waccamaw Neck for a time, but I have not located any proof as to where he may have resided.

Following the Civil War, better paying jobs and opportunities were available in Georgetown, especially in the lumber, forest products, and shipping industries. A significant number of freed slaves migrated from the plantations to the city. When the 1880 U.S. Census was taken, Renty Tucker listed his residence as 175 Orange St., Georgetown. Georgetown County land records show that Tucker purchased property described as lot #57 on the original city map. He purchased this parcel for the sum of $750.00 on March 29, 1875, from Robert E. Frazier, a successful businessman who served several terms as intendant (mayor) of Georgetown.

I found no record of a mortgage on the property. $750.00 was a considerable sum in 1875, especially considering that, by 1875, America was in the midst of the "Long Depression," that started with the "Panic of 1873" and lasted until 1879.

The property consisted of approximately 2/3 of the southeast block of Orange Street between Prince and Front Streets. The April, 1894, *Sanborn Fire Insurance Map of Georgetown* shows three frame dwellings on Tucker's property, one residence facing Prince Street and two residences facing Orange Street. He lived only one door down from Joseph Rainey, who was also born into slavery and eventually served as the first African American member of the U.S. House of Representatives. It is likely that Tucker and Rainey were acquainted, if not friends. None of the dwellings that Renty built on the property have survived. The property has since been subdivided into 4 parcels, including the lots designated today as 120, 122, and 124 Orange Street, as well as 90 feet of the rear paved parking area of the Front Street business now known as Augustus & Carolina (formerly Belks). Renty must have resided in all three dwellings at one time or another. In 1880, he was living at 175 Orange Street; in 1900, at 214 Prince Street; then in 1910, at 130 Orange Street.

IV. Renty Tucker as an Active Member of the Community

Renty found work throughout the city. The February 21, 1883, *Georgetown Enquirer* shows the county's annual report of expenditures for fiscal year 1881-1882. Renty Tucker's name appears numerous times for being paid for carpentry work performed. Subsequent issues provide evidence of disbursements for services rendered. The Duncan Methodist Church cash accounts records show Renty Tucker being paid on March 1, 1893, for repairing the church tower. The church records show several payments made in 1900 for various jobs performed. The 1900 U.S. Census shows that Tucker claimed only one month under the column for "months not employed" for the period from June 1, 1899, to May 31, 1900. Tucker was 69 in 1900, and going strong.

Renty Tucker was an involved and active member of the community. The *Fairfield Herald* (Winnsboro, SC) reported on September 20, 1876 of a mass meeting of citizens in Georgetown that was held the previous week where a "committee of safety" was formed. The article states that "The appointment of this committee was rendered necessary by the incendiary harangues of some of the Radical negro leaders of the county". [sic] This committee consisted of ten white and ten black members. Renty Tucker is listed as one of the appointees.

On October 13, 1880, the *Georgetown Enquirer* ran an ad for all Democrats on the November ballot for national, state, and local elections, with Renty Tucker as their candidate for Georgetown County Coroner. Tucker served at least a four-year term as county coroner. An article in the *Anderson Intelligencer* (Anderson Court House, SC) dated July 10, 1879, which was prior to the 1880 election, reports on a murder that occurred in a saloon in the rear of a store on Front Street. George Smith, a newcomer to Georgetown, shot Albert DeLittie. The report states that Smith and Delittie became engaged in a heated argument resulting in Smith shooting DeLittie, once in the heart and once in the skull. Coroner Renty Tucker empanelled a jury which rendered a verdict "that the deceased was killed by a pistol in the hands of George Smith, in manner and form against the peace and dignity of the state"

On June 13, 1883, the *Enquirer* reported on a murder case. Renty Tucker empanelled a jury for the purpose of an inquest. Later that year on November 14, 1883, the *Enquirer* tells of a case involving Lt. W.A. Moore of the U.S. Army Corps of Engineers, who had been in charge of the work on Mosquito Creek Canal. The article states that Moore "got into difficulty with a colored man and struck him over the head with a billet of wood" [sic]. The victim died the next day. Coroner Tucker conducted an inquest and it was determined that the victim died from a blow to the head by Moore. Tucker notified the Governor of the homicide. I found no record of a jury indicting Moore.

In addition, the *Georgetown Enquirer (05/25/1881)* reports that Renty Tucker was appointed as a member of the Board of Health by the City Council. On June 14, 1893, the *Georgetown Semi-Weekly Times* shows Renty Tucker, along with many prominent citizens, as a signer of a petition to allow a liquor dispensary to operate in Georgetown in accordance with the newly formed South Carolina Dispensary System, a state-run monopoly in liquor sales which operated from 1893 to 1907. Interestingly, the April, 1894, *Sanborn Fire Insurance Map of Georgetown* shows the "State Dispensary of Liquors" located inside an "Opera House" on the corner of Front and Orange Streets, the property adjacent to Renty's southern property line.

An obituary article in the June 26, 1913, *Georgetown Times* reports that Renty Tucker had been a member of Prince George Winyah for "upward of forty years." The *Times* article continued, saying that he served as sexton for many years (*The Charleston News and Courier* on June 30, 1913, states he was sexton for fourteen years) and, among his other duties, he was well-known for his "decorating the chancel for brilliant weddings and tolling the bell for the passing of many of South Carolina's great sons." *The Charleston News and Courier,* also on June 30, 1913, reads that; "He was always a friend of the white people, voted the Democratic ticket and was ever a willing helper in all that pertained to the best interest of the town."[sic]

Renty Tucker was instrumental in founding St.

Cyprian's Episcopal Church in Georgetown around 1895. It is a humble but quite elegant chapel with pleasing lines and proportions. Renty Tucker approached the vestry of Prince George Winyah and requested financial assistance in the construction of the chapel. The vestry did contribute, but decided to contribute as individual donors as opposed to acting as an official body of the church (*Black American Series-Georgetown County SC*, Ramona LaRoche, 2000). Apparently there was a significant enough number of African Americans who wished to continue worshiping as Episcopalians to justify building their own chapel. Renty most likely played a large role in the design and construction of the church building. The three of his sons who followed in his profession may have contributed their skills, as well.

The building still stands and can be seen at 616 Duke Street. The church was officially deconsecrated in 1998, reportedly due to financial issues. It is now privately owned and it appears that the exterior has been faithfully restored.

Renty Tucker's St. Cyprian's Episcopal Church Today, 616 Duke St. Georgetown, SC

V. Renty Tucker as a Patriarch
and Family Man

Renty and his wife Josephine reported in the 1870
U.S. Census as having ten additional household members,
children ranging from 2 years to 14 years of age. Ben,
Gabriel, Julian [St. Julian], Josey [Josiah], Peter, Summer,
Dido [Adeline], Mary, Frank, and Elizabeth. The oldest son
Ben, presumably named after Renty's father, was listed on
Tucker's 1871 bank application as "dead". He would have
been around 15 years old in 1871. Renty's wife Josephine
died in August of 1875, according to the parish records,
and she was buried on August 31, 1875, in Prince George
Parish. The well-known and beloved Rector Alexander
Glennie officiated.

Ten years later, in the 1880 Census, Renty is listed
as 49 years old and his spouse is now Diana Tucker
(45 years). There is a name "Diana" that appears on a
Weston family "slave inventory," who was working on
the adjacent True Blue Plantation prior to emancipation.
She may be the same woman who Tucker married. Parish
records also record the birth of a son, Zechariah, born on
April 30, 1876, and baptized July 12, 1876; the parents

are listed as Renty and Diana Tucker. Approximately four years later, on the 1880 Census, Zechariah does not appear, nor does he show up on subsequent censuses. There are eight additional household members recorded for 1880, ranging from ages 9 thru 20 years. The two eldest sons, Josiah (20) and St. Julian (19), were listed as carpenter and carpenter's assistant, respectively. Henry (12) is listed as his son; however, he did not appear in the 1870 Census as a member of the Tucker household. Peter, now 18, is absent. Peter ended up migrating to the Albany N.Y. area and lived until 1942, making him 80 at the time of his death. Peter still has several descendants living in that region. The child Summer, who would have been 17 in 1880, is also absent.

A new member of the household is Ella, who at 9 years, would have been Josephine's child. Ella will eventually act as his caregiver during Renty Tucker's later years.

Access to the 1890 U.S. Census would be a very helpful tool, as many Americans who are tracing family roots will tell you. Unfortunately, the 1890 Census was lost in 1921, due to fire, smoke, and water damage from a fire in the Commerce Building in Washington, D.C.

In the 1900 Census, Tucker is now 68 and married to his third wife, Nancy Tucker (née Joseph). Parish records indicate the wedding was performed on September 11, 1890, at home, and was officiated by Rev. Stewart McQueen. Besides Renty and Nancy, there are three additional household members listed in 1900; Henry Tucker (age 32), listed as carpenter; Mary Evans (née

Tucker), (age 34); and Jane Tucker (age 23). Jane is listed in the 1900 Census as "daughter-in-law," and was most likely Henry's wife. The final census that Renty Tucker participated in was in 1910, three years prior to his death in 1913. Renty was listed as age 79, and Nancy was listed as being 42 years of age. There is a discrepancy between this data and the previous Census, since she could not have lost 14 years in age. This is not due to an error in transcription, as I viewed copies of the original handwritten papers for those two years. Additional household members are Ella Jenkins (40 yrs), Modestine Jenkins (11 yrs), Ethel Jenkins (8 yrs), Nathalie Jenkins (6 yrs), and James Jenkins (4 yrs). His daughter Ella must have married and these are his grandchildren. There were at least two dwellings on the property in 1910, so perhaps Renty received some respite from the challenges of grandchildren being present.

For almost all of his adult life, Renty Tucker was surrounded by children (if the data are accurate, Renty had his oldest son Ben when he was 25, and his second son, Gabriel at 27). Renty Tucker spent almost his entire lifetime providing and parenting. He also must have been an attractive "catch," seeing that he never lacked for a spouse.

VI. Renty's Last Will and Testament, and His Funeral

Renty Tucker's health must have declined during his last year of life. The signature on his last will and testament, made about a year before his death, illustrates a weakened and feeble hand. His obituary in the *Georgetown Times*, dated June 26, 1913, mentions "...for upwards of a year had been in feeble health. He died at the home of his daughter Ella Jenkins." Fairly lengthy obituaries appeared not only in the Georgetown papers but in the Charleston and Columbia papers as well. The *Times* (June 26, 1913) reads:

> *"Renty's funeral was precisely the same as would have been given a prominent white man. Dean Robottom, pastor of the church, officiated, clothed with the vestment of his holy office. He made an address in which a strong yet sympathetic tribute was paid to old Renty's character. He spoke of Renty's honesty, faithfulness, fearlessness and devotion to duty.*

Renty's personality was impressive and his funeral illustrated the fact that sterling worth in a man is appreciated, no matter if his skin be black. A full choir of white ladies and gentleman sang at Renty's funeral. The auditorium was well filled with sons and daughters of the best families of the city and county, for the wedding of many of whose parents old Renty had rung the joy bells"* [sic].

*It is commendable and somewhat remarkable that the Editor of *TheTimes*, **Louis A Beaty**, *would* publish this statement in the segregated South during the Jim Crow era. These kinds of public acknowledgements helped to contribute to the dispelling of the stereotype. Renty Tucker's legacy helped to demonstrate that African Americans were not inherently lazy or untrustworthy.

The Parish Register of Prince George reads, "Renty Tucker (col.) the old Sexton of the Church 83 years old. Faithful and loyal Communicant. Buried with honors". The obituary in the *Georgetown Times* gives Renty credit for being a "veteran of the war of the sixties." The article also states that, "When Mr. Weston went to Columbia as Governor of the State, Renty went with him and was his valet and master of ceremonies generally." There are some historical inaccuracies in this quote. Weston acted as Lieutenant Governor for a short while, not Governor. When Weston's health was failing during the 10th Regiment's campaign in Kentucky, his friends nominated him when this position became available, allegedly so that he would not be dishonored in leaving his duty as Captain of Company A. There was not a large amount of legislative activity in Columbia during this period of The War. Weston's health continued to decline and trips to Columbia would have been arduous. *Charleston News and Courier* (June 30, 1913), indicated that Renty Tucker "pitched in," helping with the establishment of Fort Marion on South Island, where members of the Georgetown Rifle Guards became members of the Tenth Regiment of the SC Volunteers in the Confederate Army. They trained and were outfitted here prior to going into battle. It would not be unlikely for Renty to have made trips to nearby South Island to assist in construction tasks. According to S. Emanuel in *A Historical Sketch of the Georgetown Rifle Guards* (1909), as well as C.I. Walker in *Rolls and Historical Sketch of the Tenth Regiment, S.C. Volunteers* (1881) (both writers having served in the regiment); Weston's troops trained through most of 1861 in the Georgetown area. They left for Corinth, Mississippi, on April 12, 1862. Weston took a leave of duty to return home from Knoxville, Tennessee, in late October, 1862. (He was suffering from "consumption" or tuberculosis, to which he finally succumbed in 1864.)

I mention these dates to help support my belief that Renty Tucker may not have served on the front. Elizabeth Collins (1865) recorded that, "Renty being at liberty" was assigned to go to Snow Hill and restore cottages for the servants, and for several weeks, Renty and his team of carpenters were busy at Snow Hill. Snow Hill in Conwayboro (now Conway, SC) was where Emily Weston went for refuge from Union gunboats that were patrolling the lower Waccamaw River. This retreat from Hagley probably occurred in February or in the early spring of 1862

Rogers (1970) quotes a letter by Adele Allston from around 1862. She recounts that the Weston's had recently lost "their head carpenter and 18 other trusted men who had taken a large family boat and made their escape to the enemy." There is a record in a letter of R.F.W Allston's papers (S.C. Historical Society) dated March, 1863, concerning five of P.C.J. Weston's slaves making an escape. He reported that on the previous Sunday night 5 Weston slaves took a shadman's boat and started for the Federal blockade at North Island. Frank, a house servant, was among them. The escapees were never found. Occasionally diaries and letters contain hearsay as information was frequently transmitted by word of mouth. It is possible that Tucker and his crew were observed traveling to assist Weston and his troops at Fort Marion and the assumption was made that they were escapees. The problem I had with Adele Allston's account in determining if it was Renty Tucker, is that there were numerous Westons who were slaveholders in Georgetown County and she fails to mention if this was Plowden C.J. Weston. Plowden and Emily Weston's housekeeper (Collins, 1865) wrote that Renty and some of his crew assisted Mrs. Weston's transition to Snow Hill during this mass exodus of white planters from the Waccamaw and Pee Dee regions during this same time period in 1862. The appraisal of Plowden C.J. Weston's estate in 1864 listed Renty [Tucker] ,carpenter and house servant, among 15 total servants. Also based on the fact that Renty Tucker appears to have been accepted and respected in the white Georgetown community after emancipation, leads me to believe he was never considered a "turncoat".

All three of the historical accounts I have located (including the regiment's Brigadier General Manigault's writings documenting the Tenth Regiment's activities), record the use of slaves in their campaigns. Emanuel (1909), listed the names of four drum and fife corps musicians ("colored"), as well as the four Weston slaves, Flander, Caesar, Cooper, and Cudjoe, who served as a "pioneer corps," advancing ahead of the company to clear obstructions. Walker (1881) confirms this information in his accounts. Elizabeth Collins (1865), records that "The servant Hector was lost in Tennessee, but, being a clever man, he soon made his way home."

I inspected additional evidence of Renty remaining in South Carolina during the War. Emily Weston was quite a talented amateur artist, creating over 100 sketches and paintings of the South Carolina Lowcountry. She was fond of painting zoological specimens, and in two of these originals, I notice her notation, "Brought to me by Renty," referring to a native butterfly, grasshopper, and lizard. She entitled one of these pieces, "Snow Hill, 1862." Renty provided her specimens that are species most commonly found in this area during the summer months, a time in 1862 when Plowden Weston was on the battle front.

The 1910 Census was the only one that Renty participated in that asked if the person was a "Survivor of Confederate or Union Army or Navy?" The 1910 enumeration instructions for the U.S. Census taker (enumerator) were to use the initials "CA" for Confederate Army or "UA" for Union Army under column #30. On Renty's column 30 the number 3 appears and the number 7 for Nancy. (Ancestory.com resources say that the numbers appearing in the last four columns on the 1910 census were written there long after the original census was recorded. They were placed there by government office workers in preparation for recording statistics)

Renty Tucker's Last Will and Testament, dated May 7, 1912, was drafted by a prominent Georgetown attorney, Capers Barr. Reverend P. J. Robottom was named executor, and Barr as alternate executor. Renty bequeathed a one-story dwelling on the corner of Orange and Prince Streets to his daughter Ella Jenkins of Georgetown. He bequeathed a two-story dwelling to his daughter Elizabeth Kairson of Jacksonville, Florida, to have and to hold until her death, then it would be bequeathed to his beloved granddaughter, Earline Kairson.

The appraisers of the estate, H.B. Springs, James H. Fraszier, and T.L. Siau inventoried the following:

1 trunk	$ 1.50
1 wash-stand	1.50
1 bureau	6.00
3 chairs	1.50
1 book-case	12.00
Books	8.00
1 silver watch	7.50
1 bureau	2.50
1 stool chair	.50
3 chests tools	25.00
	$ 66.00
Cash on deposit in Savgs[sic]Dept. Bank of Georgetown	$ 58.45
Cash on deposit in Sav'gs[sic] Dept. Peoples Bank	$ 78.55
Total	$203.00

The *Georgetown Times* (July 26, 1913) noted that there was no mention in the will of his four sons, "St. Julian, Frank, Peter, and William."[sic]. The article reported that St. Julian was planning on joining his sister Elizabeth in contest of the will. It was said that Elizabeth, though named in the will, felt that her brothers were unfairly treated and that their father was not of sound and disposing mind when the will was signed. There is no record of papers actually being filed, and the Georgetown County Probate Court records indicate that the will was executed according to Tucker's wishes. Incidentally, there is also no mention of his wife Nancy in either the obituaries or the will. Ten years later, in 1923, his granddaughter Earline and his daughter Ella sold the property to Joseph Schenck of New York.

Renty Tucker lived a full and active life. He was a man of exceptional skill, talent, and motivation. He not only survived but he flourished through slavery, reconstruction, and segregation. In spite of the unimaginable obstacles and challenges that he must have encountered, he persevered and demonstrated an indomitable spirit. It was the hard-won success of slaves that paved the way for future generations. There must be a bittersweet feeling when learning about one's slave ancestry. I feel that it is a story that future generations must never forget.

There are many walls and stumbling blocks for African Americans tracing their history back into slavery. The people, places, and stories have become so fragmented, mainly due to how their ancestors had been treated as second-class citizens. I was able to contact and speak with one of Renty Tucker's great-granddaughters, Joyce, as well as Renty's two times great-granddaughter Sharon, both living in the Albany, New York, area. They were unaware of Renty Tucker and his accomplishments. I think this is common for many modern American families. There are very few Georgetonians who are even vaguely aware of Renty Tucker.

I spoke with someone who grew up living at Renty's "Pelican Inn" in the 1950's and 60's, as his mother owned the Inn. He had never heard of the name Renty Tucker. Though Renty and his first wife, Josephine, are both buried in Prince George Cemetery, no headstone has been found, and the Parish's current map does not indicate the burial site. Patti Burns, Head of Adult Services for the Georgetown County Library, is planning a project, utilizing the Parish archives, as well as the use of ground penetrating radar, to locate many of the unmarked graves in the Parish cemetery, with special hope in locating the Tuckers.

I think it would be fitting to one day erect a memorial stone honoring Renty Tucker. An additional way of honoring Tucker's contributions may be the recasting of the historical marker erected in front of the Pelican Inn to reflect his role in creating this historic treasure. In March, 2016 The Georgetown County Planning Commission approved our application for a street name change in Hagley. The former Clay Drive has now been renamed "Renty Tucker Court". In his wildest imagination Tucker could not have thought that one day a street appearing on "Google Earth" would bear his name.

Mr. Renty Tucker, in spite of seemingly insurmountable obstacles and a social and legal system that disenfranchised minorities, was able to achieve respect, prosperity, and success. He was not only an active participant in the community but someone who contributed to making his world a better place.

Emily Weston bequeathed to a niece her collection of over 100 sketches and paintings from her years at Hagley. This collection was later bequeathed through various descendants and ended selling at auction at Bonhams of London in 2006. A dealer from New York purchased the collection and after failing to sell it as a complete album decided to sell it as individual pieces. Dr. Hal and Mrs Margaret Holmes of Conway, SC came to the rescue and purchased the entire collection. They have since made several local lecture presentations and displayed about 50 pieces at Brookgreen Gardens. Emily made several sketches of buildings on Hagley Plantation. The main house, servants quarters, the slave village, barns, stables, a wash woman's house, are among them. Renty could have very well built some of these, but no available record exists. Emily's diary is privately owned by a different local party and is currently unavailable. This valuable document could not only document additional Renty Tucker projects but could provide additional information regarding Renty Tucker's life during his enslavement.

My Father
Peter Tucker

**Peter Tucker (1862-1942) one of Renty's sons. Peter migrated to
the Albany, NY area where he also practiced carpentry.
At least one of Peter's sons (Leon, 1898-1994) also
was a skilled carpenter.
As of this writing I have not identified any photos of Renty.
(Photo courtesy of Renty's great granddaughter,
Mrs Joyce Tucker McIntosh)**

Bibliography of Books

Bull, Henry DeSaussure, *All Saint's Church, Waccamaw : the parish, the place, the people, 1739-1968* , (1968)

Collins, Elizabeth, *Memories of the Southern States*, (1865)

Devereux, Anthony Q., *The Rice Princess-A Rice Epoch Revisited*, (1973)

Edgar, Walter B., *South Carolina A History*, (1998)

Emanuel, S., *An Historical Sketch of the Georgetown Rifle Guards and as Co.A of the Tenth Regiment, So. Ca. Volunteers in the Army of the Confederate States*, (1909)

Holcome, Brent H., *Parish Registers of Prince George Winyah Church Georgetown, SC*, (1996)

Joyner, Charles, *Down by the Riverside*, (1984)

La Roche, Ramona, *Black American Series-Georgetown County South Carolina*, (2000)

Malet, REV. William Wyndham, *An Errand to the South in the Summer of 1862*, (1863)

Manigault, Arthur Middleton, *A Carolinian goes to war: the Civil War narrative of Arthur Middleton Manigault, Brigadier General, C.S.A.,* (1983)

Pringle, Elizabeth W Allston, *Chronicles of Chicora Wood* (1976, c.1922)

Rogers, George C. Jr., *The History of Georgetown County, South Carolina,* (1970)

Walker, C.I. , Rolls *and Historical Sketch of the Tenth Regiment, So. Ca. Volunteer in the Army of the Confederate States,* (1881)

CPSIA information can be obtained
at www.ICGtesting.com
Printed in the USA
LVOW08s1521190417
531319LV00053B/120/P